CW00739755

JOHN WESL

IN

LEICESTERSHIRE

BY

JOAN STEVENSON

ROBIN STEVENSON

KAIROS PRESS
1988

Kairos Press
552 Bradgate Road, Newtown Linford
Leicestershire. LE6 0HB

Copyright © Joan Stevenson and Robin Stevenson 1988

All rights reserved
ISBN 1 871344 00 X

Printed in Great Britain by
HMC Print, Leicester

PREFACE

The late Rev Dr Leslie Newman extracted from me, a few years ago, a promise to write something about John Wesley's connection with Markfield, where Dr Newman was a minister in the 1930s. When I eventually began to tackle the project I took as a working partner my son Robin, and we broadened our canvas to cover all John Wesley's visits to Leicestershire.

A note about sources: by far the most important tools for any study of John Wesley's life are his Journals and Diaries. The Journals were written for publication, and with a few gaps cover the whole of his adult life from 1735 - 1791. The diaries were a private record, tersely recording each days activities almost hour by hour. Unfortunately they are far less complete than the Journals and have been lost for large periods of his ministry. We have also made use of many of the invaluable local church histories which are to be found in the Leicestershire Record Office.

The Illustrations are taken from contemporary engravings. The portraits are included in the 1909 edition of Wesley's Journals, and the Leicestershire scenes are from John Nichols' History and Antiquities of the County of Leicester.

We would like to acknowledge the help we have received in various ways, particularly from Roy Burchnall, Barry Biggs, Tony Squires, Eric Jarvis, Nick Horner-Maddocks, Adam Cleaver, the Revs Alan Williams, Sidney Richardson, Ivan Homer and Douglas Brewer, and the staffs of the Leicestershire Record Office, Leicester University Library and Leicester Reference Library.

Joan Stevenson
April 1988

SIGNIFICANT EVENTS	YEAR	EVENTS IN LEICESTERSHIRE
John & Charles to Georgia	1735	
	:	
John returned from Georgia	:	Mr Ellis became Rector at Markfield
JW's Aldersgate St. experiance	:	
JW's first open air service	:	
	1740	
JW's first Midlands tour	:	JW at Markfield, & Market Harborough.
JW's first tour of N. England	:	JW at Donington Park & Markfield
	:	JW at Markfield, Hinckley, Mkt Harboro'
	:	
Jacobite rebels reach Derby	1745	JW twice at Markfield
9th Earl of Huntingdon died	:	
	:	JW at Markfield for a weekend
	:	
Charles W married Sally Gwynne	:	Mr Ellis leaves Markfield Church
	1750	Lady Huntingdon leaves Donington Park
JW married Mrs Vazeille	:	
	:	
	:	JW at Markfield, and Leicester
	:	
	1755	
	:	
	:	JW in Leicester twice, & at Markfield
	:	
	:	
Death of George II	1760	
	:	
	:	
	:	
	:	JW at Ashby & Castle Donington
	1765	
	:	
	:	
	:	
	:	
	1770	JW in North West Leicestershire
	:	
	:	JW in North West Leicestershire
	:	
	:	
JW very ill, in Ireland	1775	
American Independance declared	:	Leicester Circuit formed
	:	JW at Leicester
	:	
	:	JW in Leicestershire
	1780	JW at Loughborough & Leicester
Mrs J Wesley died	:	
	:	JW at Hinckley & Leicester
	:	JW at Hinckley, Ashby, C.Don, L'boro'
	:	
	1785	
	:	JW at Mountsorrel, Leicester, Hinckley
	:	JW at Hinckley
Charles Welsey died aged 88	:	
French Revolution broke out	:	
JW's Last open air service	1790	JW's last visit to Leicester
John Wesley died, aged 88	:	

JOHN WESLEY IN LEICESTERSHIRE

CHAPTER 1

John Wesley was born at Epworth Rectory in Lincolnshire in 1703. He and his brother Charles were respectively the fifteenth and eighteenth of the nineteen children of the Rev Samuel Wesley and his wife Susanna. Less than half the children survived infancy, but despite poverty the three surviving boys, John and Charles and their elder brother Samuel, were sent to Oxford and became ordained clergymen of the Church of England.

Although John entered the church mainly to please his father, he took his religion very seriously, and he and his friends at Oxford became so diligent and methodical in their devotions that they were nicknamed Methodists. A contemporary rhyme states:

By rule they eate, by rule they drink,
Do all things else by rule, but think -
Method alone must guide 'em all,
Whence Methodists themselves they call.

In October 1735 John and Charles sailed to the American colony of Georgia. Charles stayed less than a year and was a failure; John struggled on for over two years and was a spectacular disaster. Many of the English settlers were on the run from justices or creditors at home. They did not take kindly to a straight-laced young clergyman who disapproved of slavery, lawlessness and strong drink, and who refused to marry anyone without calling the banns for three weeks beforehand. Wesley, moreover, completely mishandled a romance with the niece of one of Savannah's richest and most unprincipled citizens. When she married someone else, he refused to give her communion, was hauled before a Grand Jury on a curious selection of trumped-up charges, and finally fled the colony in danger of his life.

He returned from America a depressed and bitter man. He had put his theology to the test of life and it had failed him. Back in London, he turned to the companionship of the Moravians, who had so impressed him during the sea journey and in Savannah. He was much influenced by a Dutch merchant, Peter Bohler, in whose life he saw the love and holiness and happiness which he had found so elusive. Still a minister of the Church of England, he asked Bohler in desperation, "How can I preach to others who have not faith myself?" Bohler's advice was "Preach faith till you have it, and then because you have it you will preach faith."

On May 19th 1738 Charles Wesley had an experience of conversion. He was recovering from pleurisy when a woman who was helping to nurse him felt herself impelled to speak to him words of healing: "In the name of Jesus of Nazareth, arise! Thou shalt be healed of all thy infirmities." The healing he received was both physical and spiritual.

John Wesley's own day of deliverence followed closely. On Wednesday May 24th 1738 he opened his Bible on the words "Thou art not far from the kingdom of God." In the evening he went "very unwillingly" to Aldersgate Street, and during the reading of Luther's preface to the Epistle to the Romans, he felt his heart strangely warmed. "I felt I did trust in Christ, Christ alone, for salvation; and an assurance was given me that He had taken away my sins, even mine, and saved me from the law of sin and death." The Methodist Church dates its birth from that moment.

Three weeks after his conversion experience, John Wesley went to Germany to visit the Moravian settlements. After three months he returned to London and took up his preaching with a new zeal. At first he preached in churches, but opposition from clergy and many churchgoers began to close the doors of the churches against him. He and his brother took their message into the gaols, where the harsh penal laws of the day condemned many wretched felons to await their turn at the gallows.

The Wesley brothers were not alone in wanting to open the stifling rigidity of the Eighteenth Century

Church to the fresh air of the Gospel. George Whitefield, at 25 a preacher of great brilliance and popularity had himself drawn the opposition of the Church authorities and had responded - the church buildings being closed to him - by preaching in the open air. His first open air service, to the miners of Kingswood, near Bristol, attracted an audience of 200. His second drew 2,000, and still the crowds multiplied. The services shocked the respectable but stirred the hearts of the common people.

Whitefield was in a dilemma. He had undertaken to sail for Georgia, but he could not leave his new work at Bristol untended. So he asked John Wesley to leave London and take up his work. After some uncertainty, Wesley decided to go, but did so with trepidation. He stood beside Whitefield and gazed around at the ragged multitude with amazement. On April 2nd 1739 he held his own first open-air service, and a couple of months later Charles was led to take the same course in London.

"It pleased God," wrote St Paul, "by the foolishness of preaching to save them that believe." And preaching which didn't require walls was not confined to fixed places. It was a new, itinerant, ministry. Anywhere would serve for a pulpit where people would listen.

England was divided into a network of ecclesiastical parishes, each its incumbent's freehold. Visiting preachers were trespassers, even in the open air. The establishment began to stir in its sleep and turned its new-found energy upon the people who were turning the world upside down. All the brothers wanted was for their unconventional ministry to be accepted by the Church of England, yet the only preferment the Church ever gave them were the three years when John had acted as his father's curate, and three months when Charles acted as a curate in Islington before being driven from his post.

Wesley spent most of the rest of 1739 in Bristol, and for the next year or two he divided his time between Bristol and London, with visits to Oxford and South Wales. A spiritual revolution was beginning. During the next fifty or so years he was to travel nearly a quarter of a million miles along the roads of Britain and to preach over 42,000 sermons at an average rate of about sixteen per week. From the beginning he formed societies where those whose lives were changed could be nurtured in their faith.

The centre of Wesley's early work in London was the society in Fetter Lane, which had been founded at the suggestion of Peter Bohler. The members divided into small groups, or bands, of between 5 and 10 people which met separately twice a week and all together once a week, with a monthly Love Feast.

Among the members at Fetter Lane was a strong-minded, eccentric, aristocratic lady who was to make a distinctive contribution to coming events in Leicestershire: Selina, Countess of Huntingdon. It was quite fashionable at the time for ladies to go and hear an eloquent preacher, in the same way that they enjoyed listening to an accomplished singer or actor, but the Countess took the matter far more seriously than was considered seemly, and had appointed the young George Whitefield her chaplain. Her husband, Theophilus Hastings, 9th Earl of Huntingdon, did not share her absolute conviction, but he was happy to receive the Wesleys and other Methodists into his houses, and when in London he accompanied his wife to Fetter Lane.

Lady Huntingdon held Sunday evening gatherings when she was in town, to which she invited the Wesleys and other well-known preachers. She felt a special responsibility to present the Gospel to members of her own social class and took in her stride the derision which this earned her in sophisticated court circles. "The Queen of the Methodists got her daughter for Lady of the Bedchamber to the Princesses," crowed Horace Walpole, "but it is all off again as she will not let her play cards on Sundays." In addition, she concerned herself with the physical and spiritual wellbeing of her husband's tenants and with the education of the children on his estates.

The principal residence of the Huntingdons at

that time was Donington Park, near Castle Donington in Leicester. This mansion was described by a contemporary visitor as a 'patchwork of different periods, blazoned over with a disgusting yellow colour.' The family estates in the area were considerable despite all the land they had to sell to meet sequestration debts after the civil war, when they had been on the wrong side. They had managed to retain a great deal of North West Leicestershire, including Ashby, Loughborough, Barrow and Markfield.

Following the example of the Wesleys, Lady Huntingdon appointed her own itinerant preachers. In particular she sent her trusted coachman David Taylor, once a footman to one of her sisters-in-law, on missionary journeys in the neighbourhood of the family estates with the aim of setting up societies there. Taylor was described as "a man of ability, knowledge and wisdom, who had received a tolerable education and was called by the grace of God in truth, under the preaching of the Methodists."

On one of his preaching tours, in 1741, Taylor visited Glenfield, where curiosity brought out the villagers to hear for themselves this representative of these Methodists who were so much spoken against. A young farm worker was mowing a field near Glenfield when he heard that there was an open-air evangelist in the area and that he was to preach in the young man's village of Ratby. He immediately laid down his scythe and went to hear him. The young man was Samuel Deacon, whose family was to make its own mark on the Evangelical Revival. As a result of the impression made on him by the evangelism of David Taylor, Samuel Deacon became a preacher himself.

The clock making business at Barton-in-the-Beans (which continued until 1951 and whose workshop is now re-assembled in the Newarke Houses Museum, Leicester) was established by Samuel Deacon's son, another Samuel, who became co-pastor with his father of the little chapel there. A faithful group of Christians so built up the work that it spilled over into other parts of the county, then the Midlands, then other parts of the country, until the chapels linked together to form the New Connexion of the General Baptists. Samuel Deacon senior died in 1812 at the age of 98.

Another evangelist, Benjamin Ingham, was also active in Leicestershire, particularly in the Donington Park area. Ingham was an old friend of the Wesleys from their Oxford Holy Club days. In November 1741 he married Lady Margaret Hastings, sister-in-law to Lady Huntingdon.

BENJAMIN INGHAM

The Moravians, whom John Wesley had so much admired, had come to embrace a doctrine known as 'stillness.' Its central tenet was the need for trust in the mercy of God and total dependence on Him rather than on one's own merits. So far so good, as far as Wesley was concerned, but the proponents of the doctrine went on to follow what seemed to them a logical progression of thought: in order to depend totally on God, the seeker after salvation should sit still and do nothing! The 'means of grace,' such as going to church, taking communion, reading the Bible, praying regularly and engaging in good works, were seen to be not merely unnecessary, but undesirable.

In 1741 the Moravians visited the Donington and Nottingham areas and gained support in the societies which David Taylor and Benjamin Ingham had set up. Lady Huntingdon was alarmed by this development and is thought to have asked John Wesley to visit the area. He was determined to stamp out this seductive idea and planned his first preaching tour into the midlands.

On Monday June 8th 1741 he set out for

Leicestershire from Lady Huntingdon's London house, Enfield Chase. Wesley normally made it his practice to speak of God to everybody he met on his journeys, but this did not always come easily to him. During his two-day coach journey he decided to make an experiment which had often been urged on him - not to speak about God to anyone "unless my heart was free to it". The result was that he scarcely spoke to anyone, even his companion Mr Howard, but slept through most of the journey, and was treated throughout with unusual respect and courtesy. It was not an experiment he repeated.

After spending a night at Northampton they were on the road at 4.45, stopping for refreshment at Market Harborough. In Leicester they had dinner with Mr Craddock and his son. This may have been Joseph Craddock, a friend and kinsman of the Huntingdons, and his son Norrice. Joseph Craddock had until recently been Rector of Markfield, where Wesley was to lodge for the night with the new Rector, Edward Ellis. Mr Ellis was a good friend of the Wesleys and had been brought up and educated by Lord Huntingdon, who had appointed him to the living. While Mr Ellis was at Markfield there would be one church which would never be closed against John Wesley.

The road to Markfield was still unimproved, but Wesley still arrived in time to talk to Mr Ellis and a couple of friends for a while and then walk over to Bagworth and back before preaching at 9 o'clock. He expounded on Matthew 24 v.42 at Mr Exon's then returned to the Rectory for tea, conversation and prayer.

The following morning he wrote a letter, drank tea and preached at 8.30. At 11 he and Mr Howard set off with David Taylor. They crossed the unenclosed Charnwood Forest and ate at Long Watton at one. In the afternoon they stopped for further refreshments at Joseph Caladine's house. In his Journal Wesley describes this as being about ten miles from Markfield, and it seems to have been in the Castle Donington/Hemington area. Mr Caladine told him that a few months ago there

had been a spiritual awakening all round, but one of the Moravians had come along and three quarters of the people had gone back to sleep again.

Wesley spent a couple of days preaching in Ockbrook and Nottingham, combating the blight of stillness, and on Friday he began his journey back to Markfield with a break for tea and conversation (with which all Wesley's days were punctuated) in Loughborough. He was back in Markfield in time for more tea before preaching to a full Parish Church on "All we like sheep have gone astray..." Afterwards there was supper and prayer at the Rectory till 10.15.

The next day he was up at 5 and wrote up his Journal before preaching again at 8.15. Then he and David Taylor and Mr Clapham set off on horseback to Melbourne and Hemington, near Castle Donington. When he preached at Hemington the house was too small to hold all the people, and they had to crowd around the door and windows. An old man, known all around for his drunkenness and swearing, caught him by the hand and said "Whether thou art a good or a bad man, I know not; but I know the words thou speakest are good. I never heard the like in all my life. Oh that God would set them home upon my poor soul!" And then he burst into tears.

They spent the night at Mr Caladine's - going to bed at 10.30 and being on the road again by 5 the next morning. It was now Sunday, and after preaching in Nottingham Market Place in the morning they returned to Markfield in the afternoon. The weather was very hot and the church was crowded in every corner. Wesley had difficulty in reading the Evening Service, but when he heard that there were many people outside who had not managed to get in, he went out to them and preached again, on a different text. As there were probably only about 300 people living in Markfield at this time, such a great crowd suggests that interest had already been kindled in surrounding villages.

OPPOSITE: MARKFIELD CHURCH IN THE LATE 18th CENTURY

The following morning he was up at 4 and soon on his way to London by chaise. The only turnpike in the county at that time was the present A6, so they reached Market Harborough in time for mid-morning tea and conversation. Thus ended John Wesley's first preaching tour in Leicestershire.

LEICESTERSHIRE SHOWING SOME OF THE PLACES MENTIONED

CHAPTER 2

Although Wesley was being pressed by several people to take his message to the North of England, in the event it came about as the result of a last minute change of plan. He was in London in May 1742 when a letter arrived from Lady Huntingdon, then at Donington Park. She urged him to come at once to minister to Miss Cowper (thought to be her daughter's governess) who was dying.

He set off on Thursday May 20th, accompanied by David Taylor's brother John, whom Lady Huntingdon planned to employ as a teacher at Markfield. The journey was undertaken at Her Ladyship's expense. She provided a horse for John Taylor and probably provided Wesley's also. They reached Donington on the Saturday and found Miss Cowper just alive and greatly cheered by Mr Wesley's arrival. After staying for three days, Wesley and John Taylor moved on and embarked on Wesley's first preaching tour of Yorkshire and Newcastle. In Sheffield on their way back they met up with David Taylor, whose own evangelistic missions were attended by great numbers of people, but - as Wesley noted - he made no provision for their continued care, so most of them fell asleep again. Where David Taylor (and Benjamin Ingham) did establish societies, they mostly came to be infected by Moravian stillness.

After a month's journeying, Wesley returned to Donington Park to find that Miss Cowper had died three weeks before. He called briefly at Markfield on his return South, and arrived in London in late July to find his mother was dying. He was with her when she died and conducted her burial service.

John Wesley wasn't in Leicestershire again until November the following year, 1743. Travelling South, he called at Markfield and preached there twice in a day, then went on to Hinckley, where he records a large and quiet congregation. From there he rode to Market Harborough, where the first Methodists are thought to

have met in a thatched cottage in Adam and Eve Street, before returning to London.

On another trip to Newcastle, in February 1745, Wesley was accompanied by Richard Moss, who was at that time working at his London headquarters, the Foundery, as a servant, and who was later ordained and sent to the Bahamas as a missionary by the Bishop of London. They passed through Leicester, and soon afterwards were overtaken by a gentleman who kept them company as far as Loughborough, and dined with them there. It is thought that the gentleman was John Coltman, a Leicester hosier who had heard Wesley preach in Hinckley in 1741, and who had ridden after him with the express purpose of consulting him about his long-standing depression, which no physician could cure. Wesley talked to him of "that Physician who alone heals the broken in heart," and the gentleman rode back to Leicester, while Wesley and his companion continued North.

It was early May when Wesley came South again. He called on Saturday, at short notice, on Mr Ellis at Markfield, but word got around and the church was full for his service. He heard sadly that many neighbouring churches were ill-attended, because of the influence of the 'still brethren' who taught people that running off to church, like running around doing good works, showed lack of faith. According to his Sermon Index he preached five times at Markfield on this occasion, so it would seem he stayed over the Sunday.

From Markfield he moved to Wednesbury, where the previous year his presence had provoked serious riots. But this year he records that God had stilled the madness of the people. His opponents in Wednesbury, and other places such as Cornwall, where he headed for next, had somehow convinced themselves that the Methodists were dangerous Papists, Jesuits, supporters of Charles Edward Stewart, plotters of revolution and (at the same time) levellers of the old Puritan school. There were Methodists who died for their beliefs.

OPPOSITE: DONINGTON PARK AND HALL IN WESLEY'S TIME

Wesley called briefly at Markfield again that September, when he was travelling North again. He preached as usual to a full church in the evening, and moved on the next morning. It was a tumultuous time for the country. Charles Edward Stewart had landed in Scotland, and Wesley was anxious to be with his flock at places which were deemed to be in greatest peril during the expected march on London. He lingered at Leeds and Newcastle, but Charles chose a different route, and never reached further South than Derby.

In 1746 the circumstances of the Countess of Huntingdon changed. In October her husband Theophilus, the 9th earl, died of a stroke at the age of 49. It had been a happy marriage and Selina mourned him for the remaining 45 years of her life. Widowhood, though, brought her financial independence, for with the exception of the estates that went with the title, her husband left her, without conditions, the bulk of his large fortune. She used much of her money to set up chapels which she organised herself in a way which John Wesley (himself sometimes called Pope John in his lifetime) considered overly autocratic.

Her son Francis became the 10th earl of Huntingdon. He was a very different character from his father. After undertaking a Grand Tour with his godfather Lord Chesterfield, he cultivated a worldly, court-centred life. Being hostile to his mother's religious sentiments, he refused to consider any recommendations she made for the incumbencies of the livings of which he was Patron. Lady Huntingdon lost much of her direct influence on the people of the Hastings estates. In 1750, when her son became 21, she left him in possession of Donington Park (though he never married) and moved to Ashby-de-la-Zouch with her other children and her sisters-in-law.

John Wesley, meanwhile, continued his missionary journeys. He stopped off at Markfield again on his way South in May 1747 and preached to a well-filled church at eight in the evening. He records that God gave a blessing with his word, and the following day, a Sunday, he preached both in the morning and the evening. It is believed that the first Methodist Society was formed in Markfield shortly after this visit. The following year Mr Ellis signed the church register for the last time, and shortly afterwards moved to Osgathorpe. His successor, appointed by Lady Huntingdon's son, was George Baddely. He remained as non-resident Rector until 1791, and the Parish came under the care of a succession of curates. John Wesley paid further visits to the village, but less often stayed overnight.

In 1749 Charles Wesley married Sally Gwynne, and his ministry was thereafter confined to much

CHARLES WESLEY
Engraved from the portrait by John Russell, R.A.

narrower geographical limits. In 1751 John Wesley took the plunge into the matrimonial waters over which he had dithered several times before. His bride was a merchant's widow, Mrs Vazaille, who had three children, a fortune of £10,000, and a talent for making everyone around her miserable. Charles Wesley once wrote triumphantly to a friend that he had just spent two minutes with his sister-in-law without quarrelling once. Within a month of the marriage her chief conversation was of her husband's faults, and within a year the breach between them was public knowledge, though they did not finally part till 1778.

Such a disastrous cloud was not without its silver lining. There was no temptation for John Wesley to emulate his brother, cut down on his travelling and stop at home. There was the compensation, too, that his relationship with his wife's children seems to have been better than that with his wife. Her daughter Jane, who married a Mr Smith, sometimes accompanied him on his travels. Jane's elder daughter married a Methodist preacher, and her younger married a Swede who had been converted by Methodists. John Wesley as grandfather is a little explored aspect of his life.

CHAPTER 3

Whit Sunday 1753 was an important date for the Methodists of Leicester. On the previous day, John Wesley rode from Nottingham to Markfield, where he found time to read a tract, of which he was very critical, on the subject of Fanaticism. He preached in the church on the Sunday morning, and after dinner a gentleman arrived from Leicester and invited him to go there with him. The gentleman is thought to have been the same John Coltman who some years before had caught up with Wesley on the road to Loughborough.

They rode the eight miles to Leicester, and at 8 o'clock in the evening John Wesley preached in the town for the first time. The place chosen was an open space in Butt Close, off Churchgate. This was near to the Great Meeting, which still stands as a substantial brick chapel. Its members had a powerful influence on the town in the 18th and 19th centuries. It was built in 1708 as a joint venture between the Independents and Presbyterians, and turned Unitarian early in the next century. When Wesley began to speak people of all ranks of society came running to hear him, and he was impressed by their seriousness and attentiveness. No-one offered any interruption.

The next day he rode to Woburn, but in Leicester a Methodist Society was becoming established, and may have pre-dated Mr Wesley's visit. Mr William Lewis, a hosier of High Street, (now Highcross Street) owned a room which was licensed for public worship, and although he and his wife were members of the Great Meeting, and never became Methodists themselves, he allowed the Methodists to meet at his house. Because of the need to obtain a license from the local authority for any building or room which was to be used for non-Anglican worship, Methodists were becoming separated piecemeal from the Church of England. Wesley urged his followers to attend services at their Parish Church (where one existed, which was not the case in the new Industrial areas), to present themselves regularly for Holy Communion, and to meet in fellowship in their own Societies during the week and at times when there was no Church of England service. But to gain religious toleration and freedom of speech, they were bound to ask for a license for a Dissenting Meeting House. They didn't always feel very welcome at church, anyway. The Bishop of London had complained some years before that the Methodists and their rabble ought to leave the Church of England and declare themselves dissenters. As things stood, they thronged to the Communion table in such numbers that a clergyman scarcely had time to have dinner before the afternoon service. John Wesley always feared that "whoever leaves the church will leave the Methodists". Once they had their own buildings and the control of their own affairs, though, members who had never belonged to the established church felt their identity was Methodist rather than Anglican.

The Methodists of Leicester gained their own premises in 1753, when Mr Lewis paid £81 for an old barn in Millstone Lane, and which he presented to them. It may have been the original Grey Friars tithe barn, or a later building on the same site, and was in a ramshackle state. In its time, as well as being a barn, it had been used as a theatre, a riding school and a coal depot. The roof sagged in the middle and needed propping up, there was no ceiling, and the only light came through three small high windows or from three branched chandeliers. But it was capacious, and it was theirs. The twenty or so original members contributed sixteen shillings (80p) a quarter to Circuit funds (Leicestershire was still part of the Derbyshire Round), and Mr Coltman was one of the original trustees.

It was four years before Wesley called at Leicester again. He records, on April 14th 1757, "We rode to Leicester, where John Brandon has gathered a small society. I preached at seven; the house (supposed to contain a thousand people) was thoroughly filled. I believe there were forty or fifty soldiers, and all heard as for life."

John Brandon was a dragoon, and according to some sources, the first Methodist in Leicester. He seems to have been successful in persuading his fellow soldiers to attend the service. The 'house' was, of course, the old barn, now officially known as the Tabernacle. John Brandon became a local, and for a time an itinerant preacher, and was later active in the Ashby area. Other early Methodists in Leicester were Zechariah Siday, a schoolmaster and tailor, who was one of the first classleaders, and Jinny Sykes, a rag collector and pedlar of haberdashery, who became Siday's second wife, and who gladly offered the hospitality of her cottage to visiting preachers.

After touring the North of England, Wesley was back in Leicester on Saturday, July 30th, and preached in the evening to a large congregation. The following day he rode over to Markfield. The number of times he managed to be in Markfield on a Sunday seems to be more than a coincidence. While there was still a local pulpit to which he was welcomed, he seems to have organised his schedule to allow himself to take the prayer book services. On this occasion he preached twice. In the morning the congregation filled the church comfortably, but in the afternoon there was a great crush, and many stayed outside. The heat was stifling, and he records that he felt quite faint and weary while he read the prayers, but in preaching his strength was restored. He returned to Leicester for a six o'clock service, and "delivered my own soul."

The next time John Wesley was in the county was in 1764. On March 26th, travelling from Walsall, he arrived in the afternoon at Ashby, where the crowd filled the courtyard where he preached and the windows of the surrounding houses as well. There was only one who caused any trouble, and he, it turned out, was an attorney who lived in one of the houses adjoining the courtyard. Wesley sympathised with the man, for if everyone were to live what he preached, there would be little profit for attorneys.

The following day he rode to Castle Donington. Despite all his visits to Donington Park, this seems to have been the first time he preached in the village, though his brother Charles had been there eight years previously. A large crowd of people listened attentively while he expounded the text "God forbid that I should glory, save in the cross of our Lord Jesus Christ."

JOHN WESLEY (Aged 63)
*Engraved by Fry, from a print by Bland,
published in 1765.*

In 1768 the Leicester Methodists suffered a blow which might have deprived them of their Meeting House. William Lewis died, and it was discovered that, owing to a flaw in the original conveyancing, the property reverted at his death to his heir at law. Happily, his widow Ann was able to solve the problem by paying again the original purchase price of £81. She made sure that this time a valid contract was drawn up.

It was 1770 before John Wesley came to Leicestershire again, but this time he was able to stay for several days. Travelling from the North, he arrived in Ashby on Friday July 27th. He preached there and stayed overnight.

The following morning he rode to Castle Donington. At first the place seemed empty, because every available person was out haymaking. However, there was a sudden violent shower, which brought all the haymakers scurrying home, and he soon had a glad audience.

After a couple of days in Nottinghamshire, Wesley arrived at the village of Hoton on the evening of Monday July 30th. He compared the congregation favourably with that he had just left at Bingham, where they just gaped and stared. The Hoton folk were "more noble, behaving with utmost decency."

The following morning he was in Loughborough, preaching in the Market Place at 9 o'clock to a large and attentive audience. Thomas Pochin, who wrote a description of Loughborough in 1770, was somewhat scathing about the condition of many of the buildings. Some of the worst, he said, were owned by Lord Huntingdon and were a fire hazard because of the thatch and rotten timber. The Market Place contained a roofed Butter and Hen Cross, where farmers' wives could sell their produce sheltered from the rain; nearby were the stocks and a small prison or black hole where vagrants and disorderly persons could be confined. He notes that, besides the Church of England, there were three dissenting Meeting Houses: one for the Presbyterians, one for the General Baptists, and the other used by the followers of Wesley.

Pochin also comments that the market has got much dearer than it used to be before the recent

Enclosures took place. Agricultural improvement was sweeping the Midlands. From Loughborough Wesley had the still unenclosed Charnwood Forest to cross, but he would have found his next destination, Markfield, the scene of great changes. The previous year Parliament had granted it an Enclosure Award, with directions that the Open Fields were to be surveyed and allocated in fields to the various landowners; fences were to be built and hedges planted, and public carriage roads, sixty feet wide between the ditches, were to be created.

As at Castle Donington, the Markfield folk were out in the fields at a busy time of the farming year. However, the church quickly filled. He did not stay long, but rode into Leicester along what was now a turnpike road. On this occasion he preached in the Castle Yard, where there is now a plaque to commemorate the event. For once, someone did make an attempt to disrupt the meeting. A man was sent to shout "fresh salmon" (presumably a rare delicacy in Leicester) a little way off, but nobody took any notice of him.

LEICESTER CASTLE, WITH ITS BRICK QUEEN ANNE FACADE,
AND THE CASTLE YARD

OPPOSITE: 18th CENTURY LOUGHBOROUGH

One more sign of increasing modernity on this visit: it brought Wesley his first Press notice in Leicester. The Leicester and Nottingham Journal for Saturday August 11th 1770 wrote: "On Tuesday evening last the Rev Mr John Westley preached to a numerous audience in the Castle-Yard in this borough, but the rain prevented him from finishing his discourse - he adjourned to Wednesday morning at 5 o'clock, when he again preached to 'em in the Meeting House at the bottom of Millstone Lane."

CHAPTER 4

John Wesley planned his tours with an attention to detail which would have won the approval of Thomas Cook - another zealous Christian, who made an impression on Leicester during the next century. He normally began the day with a service at 5 a.m. so that workmen had the chance to come along before beginning their shift. Afterwards he would ride, or (particularly after he was 70) take a chaise to his next appointment, where advance notice had alerted another great crowd; and then he would move on again. So he went on, day after day, week after week, for over fifty years, except for the worst of the winter months, which he spent in London. He could be happy, settled and at home in any place.

During his visit to the Leicester area in 1772, it is possible to compare the plan of his intended visits with

THOMAS OLIVERS

those he actually made. Wesley's "Assistant" in the Circuit at that time (the equivalent of a Superintendent Minister) was Thomas Olivers, a Welsh ex-cobbler who was said to have ridden 100,000 miles on the same horse. Wesley made him editor of the 'Arminian Magazine' for a while, though he was much better at writing his own material. He is now best known as the author of the hymn "The God of Abraham praise." Five weeks before Wesley's visit Mr Olivers laid out the following plan for him:

Wednesday March	18	Burton at noon	Ashby at night
Thursday	19	Markfield	Leicester
Friday	20	Hoton	Loughborough
Saturday	21	Leek	Nottingham
Sunday	22	Nottingham; a love feast	

Monday	23	C. Donington	Derby
Tuesday	24	Crich	Derby
Wednesday	25	Ashbourne	Newcastle-under-Lyme

The visit as described in the Journal, however, was:

Wednesday March	18	Not recorded
Thursday	19	Burton-on-Trent; Ashby; Loughborough
Friday	20	Markfield; Leicester
Saturday	21	Hoton; Nottingham
Sunday	22	Castle Donington; Derby
Monday	23	Ashbourne; Macclesfield
Tuesday	24	Not recorded

Thus his visit appears for some reason to have been shortened, though he kept to the plan at least partially. 5 a.m. services don't appear on the plan; they were a bonus for the place where he spent the night.

During this visit Wesley refers to a lovely congregation in the new house at Loughborough. "Here is a fair prospect: the last society in the circuit is likely to be one of the first. They increase continually and are athirst to be, not almost, but altogether, Christians."

The next day he rode to Markfield through violent rain. Despite the weather he found the church pretty well filled with earnest listeners. In Leicester the same evening, there were other similar listeners, together with others who had little thought about saving their souls, and to whom he spoke quite differently, exhorting them to "awake out of sleep." He felt that God had applied His word, when at five the next morning, the Tabernacle, large as it was, was filled.

Leaving Leicester after the early service on Saturday, he travelled to Hoton, where he was able to preach at the house of Mrs Angrave. Before her marriage, Mrs Angrave had invited Methodist preachers into the village, but her family would not have them in the house, so they had to preach in the street. After her marriage to John Angrave in 1770 they could open there own house to them. John went on to be a leading figure in the circuit.

The following day, Sunday March 22nd 1772, they crossed Sawley Ferry in heavy rain, but it was fine all the time Wesley was preaching in Castle Donington. Here, as in Loughborough, there was a fine new Preaching House. It was considered one of the best in the neighbourhood, and the Castle Donington Society soon became one of the strongest in the area.

John Wesley did not return to Leicestershire for another five years. His ceaseless activity continued, however, except for a time in 1775 when he was very ill in Ireland and his life despaired of. In fact, his death was actually reported in one newspaper. As a result of this illness, he lost his hair and took to wearing a wig (which was very fashionable at the time anyway) for some years.

In 1776 the old 'Derbyshire Round' was sub-divided, and a Leicester Circuit was formed. Three itinerant preachers (not ministers yet) served at a time, each receiving an annual allowance of £14 plus expenses, and each stayed for two years before being moved on elsewhere. Mr Wesley's preachers were mostly very different in their social origins from those scions of the gentry who were ordained into the Church of England because they hadn't the stomach for the army or the brains for the law. When Thomas Olivers, the ex-cobbler, was in the Circuit, one of the other two itinerant preachers who served with him was Samuel Bardsley, who had been a wine-merchant's bottlewasher.

Wesley's long absences from Leicestershire may have been due to his declared policy of not just going where he was needed, but where he was needed most. Crowd trouble and violent opposition which, especially in earlier years, had brought him and his followers into physical danger in more robust areas had never been any great problem in Leicestershire. But the church has always thrived under persecution, and the areas of the most vigorous opposition erupted into the most dramatic scenes of revival: Newcastle, Yorkshire, Cornwall, South Wales... In Leicestershire the early opposition had taken a non-active, negative form: 'stillness.' This dismal doctrine carried the seeds of its own demise; what it could not do was stimulate lively reaction.

When John Wesley did next come to Leicester, on Thursday June 19 1777, he was later than intended, so the congregation had been waiting some time at the Millstone Lane Tabernacle. He therefore launched immediately into his text "Believe on the Lord Jesus Christ, and thou shalt be saved." He remarks in his Journal that he had "designed not to call here at all, supposing it would be lost labour. But the behaviour of the whole congregation convinced me that I judged wrong." After preaching to a full house again at five the next morning, he resumed his journey.

Wesley's efforts were certainly not lost labour as far as three young men from Gaddesby were concerned. They were converted on the occasion of this visit, and returned to their own village to work for the Lord. One of them, William Reeve, opened his house for Methodist preaching until he was able to build an adjoining cottage. He fitted out the lower part as the first Methodist Preaching House in the area. William Reeve lived to be nearly 100 and was a class leader for 60 years. His family were active in Methodist affairs for several generations, and his great-grandson came back to the Circuit as a Minister, when he was delighted to be entertained in the house where his great-grandfather had held the first Methodist services in Gaddesby. William Reeve and his friends heard Mr Wesley again, on his last visit to Leicester, when Wesley, his eyesight failing, recognised them by their voices.

On Saturday July 17th 1779, John Wesley preached at noon in Castle Donington. Because of the heat he chose to stay in the open air. One of the people present was Mrs Bowman, who afterwards became a class-leader for many years in the very active Castle Donington Society.

Wesley spent Sunday in Nottingham, and after a 5 a.m. service there on the Monday morning, he was in

OPPOSITE: 18th CENTURY HINCKLEY

Loughborough Market Place at nine, in Griffydam about noon, and in Ashby in the evening.

The following day he preached at Markfield about noon, and in the evening he was in Leicester, where, he records, "we had an exceeding solemn time while I described the Son of Man coming in his glory."

On the Wednesday morning the Preaching House was filled for his 5 a.m. service, after which he set off southwards. Reaching Hinckley about 8, he was asked to preach before continuing towards Coventry. This was his second visit to Hinckley, the first being in 1744.

It was just about a year before Wesley was back in the county. Travelling South from Nottingham, he preached at Loughborough at 11 o'clock in the morning on Wednesday July 5th 1780. Afterwards he went on to Leicester and preached there in the evening, writing in his Journal "I know not how it is that I constantly find such liberty of spirit in this place."

The next morning, the room was filled from end to end for his 5 a.m. service. "I have not spent a whole day in Leicester for these last fifty-two years," he wrote. "Surely I shall before I die."

It was July again, two years later in 1782, when John Wesley, now 79 years old, made a detour into Leicestershire on his way from Birmingham to London. According to his Journal, he preached at Hinckley on the evening of Monday July 15th, calling it "one of the civilest towns I have seen." The next Journal entry is for the Wednesday, when he records merely "I went on to Leicester."

Perhaps during that visit to Hinckley he was asked to return the next year to open their first chapel. Until that time services were held in a large room at the back of some houses at the top of Stockwell Head. John Wesley arrived by chaise on Thursday March 27th 1783, on a circuitous journey from Bristol to Ireland. He had been ill with a fever until a few days before, and had

had to ask a supportive clergyman to take his appointments. When he recovered, he took a chaise and caught up with his schedule. He writes "I crossed over the country to Hinckley, and preached in the evening in the neat, elegant preaching-house. So I did, morning and evening, on the three following days to a serious, well-behaved people."

Wesley makes no mention of opening the new Preaching House, but it is an oral tradition that he did so, staying with Mrs King and her son John. Three days was an extended sojourn by his standards, longer than he ever spent anywhere else in Leicestershire.

He doesn't seem to have visited Leicester on this occasion, but went on to Ashby, where he held a love feast and spent some time writing up his Journal. Then he went to Castle Donington.

On his way back from Ireland, on May 27th, he preached at Loughborough in the morning and Mountsorrel at 1 p.m. While he was preaching, it began to rain. This was much needed, but continued non-stop for the next two days. In the evening he preached at Leicester "where I always feel such liberty, and yet see but little fruit." He preached there again early the next morning, then resumed his journey South.

Three years later Wesley again passed through Leicestershire while travelling South. On Monday July 10th 1786 he left Nottingham after his early morning service and by 9 o'clock he was preaching in Mountsorrel on Romans 1, 16. He noted that although it was fair day he did not see one drunken person in the congregation.

It rained most of the way to Leicester, so that some feared no-one would turn out to hear him. "Vain fear!" he exclaims. "The preaching house was extremely crowded with deeply attentive hearers, while I applied our Lord's words to the Centurion, in effect spoken to us also, "As thou hast believed, so be it done unto thee."

The rain continuing, he travelled on to Hinckley

in the afternoon and preached there at 6.30. The new preaching house was overflowing, and a more serious, well-behaved people he reckoned he had seldom seen. While he was preaching, a man in the street, while cursing another, called upon God to "blast his eyes". He was immediately struck blind, and remained so for the time being.

After an 8 o'clock supper and more time in prayer, Wesley retired for the night at 9.30. The following day he was up at 4 and in Coventry by 11. Later in the month Conference met in Bristol and a chief item for discussion was separation from the Church of England. It was agreed, wrote Wesley, "to remain therein - at least until I am removed to a better world."

CHAPTER 5

Long distance travel became somewhat easier in the mid 1780s. The old heavy, badly sprung stage coaches carrying six inside passengers and more outside, were replaced by faster, more comfortable vehicles, which carried four inside passengers and an armed guard against highwaymen. Every seven or eight miles there was a swift change of horses and this enabled journey times to be cut dramatically. Although the turnpike roads still awaited McAdam's superior surfacing, regular time-tables of coaches soon linked the major towns.

In February 1787 John Wesley made what appears to be his first journey on one of the new mail-coaches. The Post Office initially opposed the idea of their vehicles carrying passengers as they feared attacks on the mail. However, no mail-coaches were ever robbed in England, and they had the advantages of extra speed and a strict time-table.

The reason for Wesley's journey was a request from the society at Newark to open their new Preaching House. He accordingly took the mail along the Great North Road - part of the London-York-Newcastle service. He and his companion left London on the evening of Friday, February 9th, and reached Newark - a distance of 124 miles - the following afternoon. The following day he preached in the new chapel in the presence of the Mayor and some of the aldermen.

On the Monday he wished to return to London, but there were no places to be had on the coach from York. He and Mr Broadbent, with whom he was travelling, therefore decided to take a route across country. Stopping briefly at Nottingham and Leicester, they arrived late in the afternoon at Hinckley. The people had no prior notice of his coming, but word soon got around and, although it was raining, the preaching-house quickly filled and he preached to them at 6.30. Many, he believed, were filled with peace and joy in the Holy Ghost.

While he was in Hinckley, Wesley enquired about the man who had been struck blind the previous year. He was told that he had remained in that condition for some time, but as soon as he recovered his sight he had lapsed into being as profane as he had before.

While he was in Hinckley he wrote a letter to Joseph Taylor, one of his itinerant preachers who had been in the Leicester Circuit in 1777, warning against long services and the 'spinning out' of sermons. The next morning he was up at 4, preached at 6, and spent the morning in conversation before continuing on his way "leaving the society here very much alive in God."

He was now 83 years old and noted that he still weighed 9 stone, just as he had in his youth. Although he was only 5 feet 3 inches tall, all who saw him found him striking in appearance.

Some time during 1787 the Tabernacle in Leicester was taken down and replaced on the same site by a purpose-built chapel to hold 400. On the opening day the preacher was the Rev Dr Thomas Coke, but the evening service had to be held in the Great Meeting, which was larger.

The last few weeks of 1787 were dramatic ones for Leicester. John Coltman had joined with Joseph Whetstone and Joseph Brookhouse (all members of the Great Meeting) to exploit a new means of worsted spinning which Brookhouse had invented. At this time hosiery was virtually the only manufacturing industry in Leicester and most of the county, and knitters and their families were working 15 hours a day to keep themselves scarcely above starvation level.

New inventions which cut down on labour were inevitably greeted with hostility, and on the evening of December 1st an angry mob attacked Mr Whetstone's house. Then they went on to Mr Coltman's and smashed his windows before returning to Mr Whetstone's. He fired into the crowd, causing at least one person to be taken off to the Infirmary. The Mayor eventually arrived and read the Riot Act, and in due course the crowd was subdued.

The next night, though, there was more violence. This time the Mayor was hit by a stone thrown by one of the rioters while he was trying to read the Riot Act, and eventually died of his injuries. The Militia was sent for, but the rioting went on for ten days.

The ineptness of the Corporation's response to the riots was matched by its solution to the problem. It banned the use of the new spinning machine in the town - so Joseph Brookhouse took it off to Warwickshire when it might have provided work in Leicester.

The root of Leicester's problem was its reliance on one overcrowded and unstable industry, and this was not tackled until the middle of the next century. Its effects were exacerbated by a rift between the more forward-looking manufacturers, who were by and large Liberal Nonconformists (mostly from the Great Meeting), and the self-perpetuating Corporation, who were Anglican Tories. Thus, when the hosiers' houses were attacked, the Corporation delayed their reponse to appeals for assistance, and in the aftermath they took the side of the rioters. Leicester was divided against itself, and John Wesley in his Journal seems to have sensed the town's lack of direction. He had declared in 1777 that he hadn't intended to stop there at all, supposing it would be lost labour (though admitting afterwards that it had not been so). Wesley's own influence played its part in the re-awakening of spiritual and political vitality which took place in the next century, when the old corrupt Corporation was swept away and the Nonconformists were in the forefront of civic activity.

In 1788 Charles Wesley died. John, aged 85, was still travelling thirty to forty miles a day, and covering a large part of England and Wales each year. He was loath to admit to any infirmities of his own, but acknowledged that he could no longer easily preach more than twice a day, or write for more than 15 hours in the day without hurting his eyes. In his remaining years it was his declining eyesight which was his chief disability.

The gradual distancing of most Methodists from the Church of England was to some extent offset by the entry into the Anglican priesthood of men who had been influenced or converted by Wesley's preaching, and who were keen to rekindle the church from within. One such was Dr Ford, who was born in Bristol in 1742 and who early in life was converted through the work of John Wesley. He became Vicar of Melton in 1773 and remained there for 47 years, gaining a reputation for evangelical fervour. He many times invited Wesley to preach in Melton, but his priorities were elsewhere where the need was greater. In reply to such an invitation in 1789, Wesley wrote to Dr Ford:

Dear Sir,
It would have been a great pleasure to wait upon you at Melton Mowbray, but at the present it cannot be, as I am engaged to be at Newark on Wednesday, at Hinxworth on Thursday, and at London on Friday. Wishing every blessing to Mrs Ford and you.
I am, dear Sir, your affectionate brother,
John Wesley

Methodism was not strong in Melton Mowbray, which was not surprising in a place where the Vicar himself undertook the kind of work usually left to the Methodists. There was a Methodist Society in existence in 1779. Two of the first members were James and Ann Brown. Apparently attending Methodist services still brought the risk of abuse from some sections of the town, for James Brown would sometimes suggest they went home by a back way to avoid being noticed. His wife would then remonstrate briskly, "Nay, Jimmy. There's no back way to heaven." In 1781 a Mr Tyler came to live in the town and opened his house for Methodist services and for the accommodation of preachers. Later he moved to London and, although the Browns struggled

OPPOSITE: LEICESTER CASTLE & ST. MARY DE CASTRO IN THE 1790s

to keep the society going for a year, it had to close for lack of members. The Browns then travelled two or three times a week to Frisby, and James Brown was also a class leader in Great Dalby. Happily, he lived to see the work in Melton resumed and the first Methodist Chapel erected there in 1796.

Leicester also had a 'Church Methodist' in the person of Thomas Robinson, Vicar of St Mary de Castro for many years from 1778. He and the Rev Robert Hall, the Baptist minister who succeeded William Carey at Harvey Lane Chapel, worked together on many projects and between them made a great impression on the spiritual life of the town.

Another such Anglican was Walter Sellon, one of the earliest Methodist preachers, who was for a time the schoolmaster at Kingswood School in Bristol, where the sons of itinerant preachers were educated. He was later ordained into the Church of England and became curate of Breedon-on-the-Hill from 1759-71 and then at Smisby among other places. He attracted large crowds to his services, and engaged in evangelistic activities in nearby villages.

Mr Sellon was a great friend of Rev John Fletcher, Wesley's heir apparent who unfortunately predeceased him. John Fletcher used to preach sometimes at Breedon and huge crowds would gather to hear him. At one time, it seems, the church caretaker tried to collect a penny from everyone who was not a member of the normal congregation, but he was discovered and made to pay it all back.

While at Breedon Walter Sellon lodged with Mr John Hall of Tonge, whose sister Mrs Skirmer opened her cottage as the first preaching house in the village. After her death Mr Hall, who had been converted while taking communion at Breedon church, allowed his house to be used.

It is thought to have been John Hall who took Wesley to Griffydam, though it is not recorded in the

Journal. The story is that the local squire determined to break up the meeting, so he treated his colliers liberally with drink and armed them with truncheons. To lead them he chose a noted pugilist named John Massey, who was considered the terror of North West Leicestershire. After some hymns and prayers Wesley started to preach. Massey was about to launch an attack, but decided to listen first. As a result he was converted, and instead of calling his fellow miners onto the rampage, he told them that anyone who tackled Wesley would have him to deal with the next day.

John Massey became a well-known local preacher and drew large crowds to his own services till he died in 1819 at the age of 87. On one occasion he stood in for John Fletcher, who had not arrived at Mr Hall's when the service was due to start. The room was packed, and when Mr Fletcher finally arrived he listened, and later congratulated Mr Massey on his sermon. The first chapel at Griffydam was built in 1778 and enlarged in 1792. Its membership now is tiny, but its famous Love Feasts have been a pilgrimage of grace to many.

One of the regular attenders at Walter Sellon's church at Breedon was a man from Wymeswold who walked the three hour journey in time for the morning service all the year round. He became a well-known local figure as he tramped the lanes with his coat slung over his shoulder, often wiping the perspiration from his brow. His name was never recorded, but he was probably one of the founders of the Methodist Society in Wymeswold, which seems to have been in existence by 1771.

The strength of Wesley's mission lay not in his ability to draw large crowds, but in the way that his converts took upon themselves his task of spreading scriptual holiness throughout the land. Methodist societies took root in towns and villages which had never entertained Mr Wesley, and were led for the most part by men and women of little education and no social standing.

One such was Benjamin Squire, who introduced Methodism to Woodhouse Eaves. The first Methodist preacher he heard was the Yorkshire stonemason John Nelson, who had been stationed as an Itinerant preacher in the Circuit in 1768. After hearing John Nelson at Markfield, Benjamin Squire began to travel far and wide to hear Mr Wesley, George Whitefield, and other preachers. He felt a conversion experience one night as he walked home from Mountsorrel, and began to invite Methodist preachers to use his own humble cottage. He would climb the nearby hills to watch for their arrival, musing on the words of Isaiah, "How beautiful upon the mountains are the feet of him that bringeth good tidings." He held weekly meetings at his house until he died in 1820 at the age of 95, a revered old servant of the Lord.

John Wesley's last visit to Leicester, in 1790, was long remembered in the town. He came as the guest of John Rawson, one of the trustees of the new chapel. The expense of this section of his journey was borne by the Circuit, who paid £1.6s.0d. "for Mr Wesley's carriage through the circuit." He preached on the first verse of the 33rd Psalm. As he passed along the street, he replied to those who spoke to him by saying "Little children, love one another." There were election riots in Leicester that year, and in France a full-scale Revolution...

A description of him at that time observes "A clear, smooth forehead, an aquiline nose, an eye of the brightest and most piercing that can be conceived... In dress, he was a pattern of neatness and simplicity. A narrow, plaited stock, a coat with a small upright collar; no buckles at his knees; no silk or velvet in any part of his apparel, and a head as white as snow, gave an idea of something primitive and apostolic; while an air of neatness and cleanliness was diffused over his whole person."

There is a gap in Wesley's Journals for the months of July and August 1790, but his visit to Leicester is tersely recorded in his diary. The month is July, and he begins the day in Nottingham.

Sunday 11th
4 Prayed, Mag.; 8 tea, conversed, prayer; 9.30 prayers, Matt.v.3, (undeciphered); 1 dinner; 2 chaise;

5.30 Leicr, tea; 6 Psa. xxxiii.1; 7.30 supper, conversed, prayer; 9.30.

Monday 12th
3 Tea; 4 coach; 8.30 tea,coach; 2 Dunstable, dinner; 3.30 coach; 7.30 London, within, supper, conversed, prayer; 9.30.

John Wesley died in London the following year, on March 2nd 1791 in his 88th year. He was an honoured name now, active almost to the end, and planning another trip to Ireland. His friends gathered round him and almost his last words were "The best of all is God is with us."

THE DEATH BED OF JOHN WESLEY

BIBLIOGRAPHY

LRO - Leicestershire County Record Office
TLAHS - Transactions of the Leicestershire
    Archaeological and Historical Society

Baker, Frank, A Charge to Keep, Epworth, 1947
Barton Church Magazine January 1892
Biggs, B.J, In the Heart of the City, pr Alfred A
    Taberer, 1965
Biggs, B.J, The Wesleys and the Early Dorset
    Methodists, Woodsorrel Pub. 1987
Birrell, Augustine, John Wesley, Some Aspects of the
    18th Century in England, 1899 rep Epworth 1938
Brownlow, Jack, Centenary of 2nd Sage Cross Central
    Methodist Church, Melton, 1971, LRO
Dictionary of National Biography
Fielding Johnson, Mrs T, Glimpses of Ancient
    Leicester, J & T Spencer, 1891
Fitchett, W.H, Wesley and his Century, Smith, Elder
    & Co., 1906
Green, George H & M.W, Loughborough Markets and
    Fairs, Echo Press, 1964
Harrison, A.H.W, History of Wesleyan Methodism in
    Castle Donington, LRO
Harrison, Fred M.W, It All Began Here E. Midland
    Baptist Assoc 1986
Hastings Manuscripts, Vol III, Historical MSS
    Commission, 1934, LRO
Heather Methodist Church, 1828-1978, LRO
Hinckley Past and Present (Story of Early Leic.
    Methodism), Methodist Recorder 1903, LRO
Jarvis, Eric, The Whitwick Methodists, 1988
Keen, Tom, History of Wesleyan Methodism in
    Hinckley, 1928, LRO
Kirby, Ralph (ed), Methodist Bedside Book, Hulton
    Press, 1954
Laine, J.A, Methodism in and around Leicester, pr
    W Thornley, c.1956
Lean, Garth, John Wesley, Anglican, Blandford Press,
    1964

Leicester and Nottingham Journal, 1770,
Mann, Stuart, Methodism and the Industrial
     Revolution, 1979 unpub.
Markfield Enclosure Award 1769, LRO
Martin, Victor H, Market Harborough Methodist Church
     1871-1971, 1971, LRO
Nichols, John, History and Antiquities of the County
     of Leicester, repub S.R. Publishers, 1971
Pochin, Thomas, Loughborough in 1770, rep
     J.D.Bennett, 1970
Register of Deaths in the Loughborough Circuit,
     1804-1820, LRO
Richardson, S.Y, Methodist Ministers in Circuit
     1765-1899, LRO
Richardson, Rev Sidney Y, Methodism in Wymesworld,
     1985, LRO
Seymour, Aaron Crosley Hobart, Selina Hastings,
     Countess of Huntingdon, 1840
Simmons, Jack, Leicester, the Ancient Borough to
     1860, Alan Sutton, 1983
Tytler, Sarah, The Countess of Huntingdon and Her
     Circle, Pitman, 1907
Ward, Rev J, Sketches of Wesleyan Methodism in
     Melton Mowbray, Pr J Towne 1874, LRO
Wesley, John, The Journal, ed Nehemiah Curnock (8
     vol), Epworth, 1909
Winchester, C.T, The Life of John Wesley, Macmillan,
     1906
Wykes, David A, The Leicester Riots of 1773 and
     1787, TLAHS, 1987-9, LRO

INDEX